INSPIRATIONAL LIVES

AMIR KHAN
CHAMPION BOXER

Clive Gifford

WAYLAND

Updated and published in paperback in 2017
by Wayland
Copyright © Hodder & Stoughton Limited,
2017

Wayland is an imprint of
Hachette Children's Group
Part of Hodder & Stoughton
Carmelite House, 50 Victoria Embankment
London EC4Y 0DZ

Editor: Nicola Edwards
Designer: Paul Cherrill for Basement68

British Library cataloguing
in Publication Data
Gifford, Clive.
Amir Khan -- (Inspirational lives)
   1. Khan, Amir, 1986- --Juvenile literature.
   2. Boxers (Sports)--Great Britain
   --Biography--Juvenile literature.
I. Title II. Series
796.8'3'092-dc23

ISBN: 978 1 5263 0126 0
10 9 8 7 6 5 4 3 2 1

Printed in China

Wayland is a division of
Hachette Children's Group,
an Hachette UK company.

www.hachette.co.uk

Picture acknowledgements:
The author and publisher would like to thank
the following for allowing their pictures to
be reproduced in this publication: Cover
AFP/Getty Images; p4 AFP/Getty Images;
p5 Getty Images; p6 PA/PA Archive/Press
Association Images; p7 Simon Dawson/AP/
Press Association Images; p8 Getty Images;
p9 Getty Images; p10 PA/PA Archive/Press
Association Images; p11 Getty Images; p12
AFP/Getty Images; p13 David Davies/PA
Archive/Press Association Images; p14PA/
PA Archive/Press Association Images; p15
Getty Images; p16 Dave Thompson/PA
Archive/Press Association Images; p17 Nick
Potts/PA Archive/Press Association Images;
p18 Dave Thompson/PA Archive/Press
Association Images; p19 Dave Thompson/
PA Archive/Press Association Images; p20
Getty Images; p21 Getty Images; p22 Getty
Images; p23 Getty Images; p24 Featureflash
/ Shutterstock.com; p25 Eamonn and James
Clarke/Eamonn and James Clarke/EMPICS
Entertainment; p26 AFP/Getty Images; p27
Anthony Upton/PA Archive/Press Association
Images

Contents

World Champion!

"Seconds out. Round one." As the **ring announcer's** words faded in the air and the crowd roared, Amir Khan began the biggest fight of his life. Khan was taking part in his first ever world championship boxing **bout**. What's more, he was in front of a large home crowd as the young British boxer was fighting in the Manchester Evening News (MEN) Arena, just 30 kilometres from his home town of Bolton.

WOW!

Khan became the third youngest British world boxing champion of all time with his victory in 2009.

Boxing is divided into different **weight divisions** so that boxers of roughly equal weight and size fight each other. To fight the WBA light welterweight champion, Andreas Kotelnik, Amir had had to move up a weight division. Previously he had fought in the lighter lightweight division. Amir's opponent was from the Ukraine. Kotelnik was a tough, rugged boxer and a veteran of over 30 professional fights.

Amir fires a right **jab** punch through the guard of Andreas Kotelnik. Amir landed 170 punches throughout the fight, while Kotelnik managed only 80.

4

Urged on by a raucous 10,000 strong crowd at the MEN Arena, Khan kept the audience excited with an all-action display. With lightning-fast reactions, he moved forward, punched quickly and nimbly stepped out of range of many of Kotelnik's punches. Yet the young challenger did not have things all his own way. There were anxious times among Amir's family and his training team in the ninth round, for example, when he was hit hard several times. But Amir stood firm and completed all 12 rounds of the fight.

When a boxing bout ends with both fighters still standing, it is up to the judges to decide who is the winner. All three judges gave the fight to Amir by wide margins – 120-108, 118-111 and 118-111. He had become the World Boxing Association light-welterweight champion. He was only 22 years old. "It's the best feeling ever," said Khan afterwards. "I'm a world champion and I'm going to enjoy it. I'm still young and I've got big things to come."

Amir Khan holds the WBA light-welterweight world championship belt after his historic victory against Andreas Kotelnik on the 18th July 2009.

INSPIRATION

In interviews after the fight, Amir credited his **trainer**, Freddie Roach with helping him to cut out errors in his boxing and develop into a more **professional** fighter. He was also inspired by one of Roach's other fighters, the many times world champion Manny Pacquaio.

A happy childhood

Amir Iqbal Khan was born in Bolton in 1986. He was a tiny, sickly baby and suffered an infection that kept him in hospital for weeks after his birth. He soon grew into a lively, likeable and excitable young boy, even though his parents thought he sometimes had too much energy and stubbornness for his own good.

Amir remembers his childhood as being a very happy one. He grew up in Bolton, in the northwest of England. His family consisted of his mother, Falak, his father, Shah, two sisters, Mariyah and Tabinda, and a younger brother, Haroon. Living close by was Amir's Uncle Shahid and his family, which included Sajid Mahmood, the England fast bowler. Amir and Sajid would often play cricket in the streets as children. Amir could strike the ball fiercely as a batsman, although he and Sajid agree that Amir didn't have the patience to really prosper at cricket.

Four-year-old Amir smiles like an angel but was already getting into trouble. Before he reached his fifth birthday he ran across a road whilst at a wedding and was run over by a car.

INSPIRATION

Despite his early scrapes, Amir is still extremely close to his parents and even in 2009 was living at home. "My parents still tell me off," he says, "and I still respect them for doing it."

In fact, Amir as a young boy had very little patience but plenty of daring. He was often getting himself into scrapes, once eating the cake on the teacher's desk whilst at Brownlow Fold Primary School and climbing up the drainpipe of his family's house and onto the roof when he was only five.

As he grew a little older, he found himself getting into fights, often with bigger boys than himself as his reputation as a fearless brawler began to increase at school. His parents would often be forced to punish Amir by grounding him. In interviews, Amir remembers those times as especially painful as all he wanted to do was spend time outdoors using up his vast reserves of energy.

*Amir celebrates another win with his family, including his father, Shah (far right). The two have remained close throughout Amir's **amateur** and professional boxing careers with Shah attending his fights and working behind the scenes for Amir.*

WOW!

As a teenager at Smithills School, Amir won local 1,500m track athletics championship titles.

Bolton boy

Amir's family tree stretches back into Rawalpindi in Pakistan. His grandfather, Lall Khan, came from there to England in the 1960s to make a new life for his family. Lall Khan's three sons, Shahid, Tahir and Shah (Amir's father) would all settle in or around Bolton. Shahid, known as Terry, would become a policeman, Tahir an IT expert and Shah would run a scrap metal dealership.

Amir was brought up as a Muslim and as an adult, continues to strive to live by the teachings laid out in the Koran. He does not drink alcohol or smoke cigarettes and strives to study parts of the Koran every day. He also donates his time and money to charities, at home in Bolton and internationally.

Amir stands with his mother, Falak, father, Shah and younger sister, Mariyah at the opening of the Gloves community centre in Bolton. It is one of a number of local projects that Amir feels strongly about and supports.

INSPIRATION

In a television interview, Amir explained how his Muslim faith inspires him. He said: "It tells me the rights and wrongs in life. My faith also helps me to focus, and gives me that strength in what I do."

Amir remains extremely proud of his religion and Asian roots but also his upbringing as a son of Bolton. Although he travels widely around the world and trains mostly in the United States, he would always swap the glitz and glamour of cities like New York and Los Angeles for his home town. Amir finds Bolton a friendly place and returns to whenever he can.

Amir Khan's **autobiography** was called *A Boy From Bolton* and in an interview in 2011, he explained one of the reasons why he is so proud to be British. "The great thing about Britain is that we give everyone a chance. People love to talk Britain down, but we let a lot of people come here, work here, live here, from violent countries like Iraq and Afghanistan, and find some peace in their lives. And that's what makes us a special country, and we should be proud of that."

Amir greets a fellow fan at Bolton Wanderers' Reebook Stadium. Amir and his fiancé, Farya Makhdoom, had their engagement party at the ground of his childhood team in 2013.

Starting boxing

It was Shah Khan's idea to first take his eight-year-old son to a boxing club housed in the basement of a disused Bolton factory to find a positive, safe outlet for his relentless energy. It proved an inspired decision. Amir's first coach was the aptly-named, Tommy Battle. He used to tie up the battered old boxing gloves in the Halliwell Boxing Club using shoe laces. At first the large gloves felt heavy and clumsy on Amir's small hands, but he quickly got used to them.

Amir the schoolboy, aged 16. Amir's parents released this picture to the press when Amir began to do well at the Athens Olympics and everyone wanted to know more about the boy from Bolton.

Khan proved to be a rapid learner and a highly skilled raw talent. He fell in love with boxing, watched as many bouts as he could on TV and started pestering his parents for his own gloves, skipping rope and other training aids. He was really upset when the Halliwell club closed and took up **karate** for a year until he was old enough at almost eleven to attend another local boxing gym, the Bolton Lads club.

TOP TIP

Amir learned quickly to concentrate and follow his coach's instructions. By channelling all his energy into training in and out of the gym, Amir was able to stay out of trouble, do better at school and get seriously fit so that his boxing improved.

Amir had his first competitive fight three days after his eleventh birthday against Mark Jones in Stoke-on-Trent. He won the three-round fight convincingly but would suffer a number of defeats as he came up against bigger and more experienced boys.

WOW!

When he was 14 years old and watching a boxing tournament in Manchester, Ricky Hatton asked for Amir's autograph!

Amir's father decided that a change of gym would benefit his son. They settled on the Bury Amateur Boxing Club in 1998. Although the building was small and tatty, the man who ran it, Mick Jelley, was larger than life. He would guide Amir through his amateur career which took off with a run of 17 unbeaten fights between 1999 and 2000 and later resulted in Amir becoming England Schoolboys and ABA junior champion in the lightweight division. Amir's fights were drawing large crowds and a lot of attention from amateur boxing experts. But most thought that the 2004 Olympics would come too early for him. They would be proven wrong.

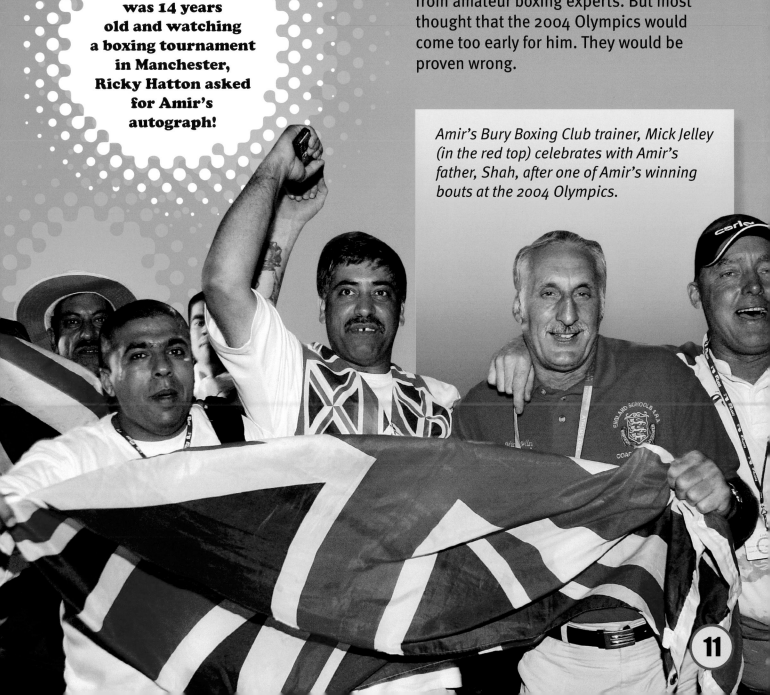

Amir's Bury Boxing Club trainer, Mick Jelley (in the red top) celebrates with Amir's father, Shah, after one of Amir's winning bouts at the 2004 Olympics.

Amir the Olympian

The 2004 Olympics were held in Athens, Greece, a four-hour flight from the UK. But Amir had to travel a lot further in his bid to qualify as an Olympian, and claim his place at the pinnacle of amateur boxing. He flew to the US state of Louisiana in 2003 to take part in the Junior Olympics, where he won gold. This was followed by tournaments in Lithuania, South Korea and finally Bulgaria. There, at the 1st AIBA Olympic qualifying tournament, Amir won his Olympic place.

Amir was only 17 when he boarded the flight bound for Athens and the 2004 Olympic Games. No other British boxer had qualified in any of the other weight divisions, so it was just him and the Team GB boxing coach, Terry Edwards.

However, Amir wasn't short of support, as his uncle Tahir had arranged for more than a dozen friends and family to fly out.

Amir Khan punches his Olympic semi-final opponent Serik Yeleuov. Amir's win guaranteed him a silver medal.

INSPIRATION

One of Khan's boxing heroes, Muhammad Ali, won an Olympic gold medal in the light-heavyweight division at the 1960 Olympics.

Amir defeated local favourite Marios Kaperonis in the first round of competition before beating the European lightweight champion Dimitar Stilianov by 16 points. Even better was to come with Amir's victory over South Korea's Jong Sub Baik – the **referee** stopped the fight in the first round. After two of the four rounds of his semi-final bout, Amir was behind on points against Serik Yeleuov of Kazakhstan. He rallied to win and reach the final where he faced Cuba's Mario Kindelán.

Kindelán was 16 years older than Amir and the reigning Olympic champion and 2003 world champion. Amir was confident going into the fight but as the four rounds progressed, Kindelán always seemed to be one step ahead. The judges awarded the fight 30-22 to Kindelán. Amir was hugely disappointed at first, but to win an Olympic silver medal at just 17 was an extraordinary achievement.

WOW!

In Amir's autobiography, he reveals that US boxing officials tried to persuade him to switch nationalities to fight for the USA at the 2004 Olympics. He turned them down.

Amir stands on the **podium** wearing his Olympic silver medal and a crown made of olive leaves.

A hero's return

Amir returned from Athens to Britain to find his world had changed. When he'd arrived at the Olympics he'd been relatively unknown. Media interest and crowd support had increased throughout the competition but nothing could prepare him for the frenzy that greeted his return.

Large crowds gathered outside his home, while inside the phone was ringing off the hook. It seemed that every newspaper, radio station and TV channel wanted photos, quotes and interviews from the fresh-faced boxer.

Amir, friends and family enjoy the open-topped bus parade around Bolton shortly after his return from the Athens Olympics.

Amir was invited to many events including a Downing Street reception where he met Prime Minister Tony Blair. Most daunting of all was a visit to Buckingham Palace. Amir said he was more nervous meeting the Queen than facing some of his opponents! He was stunned to learn that the Queen had watched some of his fights. The Queen congratulated Amir on doing so much for the country.

WOW!

Before the Olympics, the Amateur Boxing Association (ABA) paid Amir just £10 a week. Suddenly, sponsorships and other business deals were worth tens of thousands.

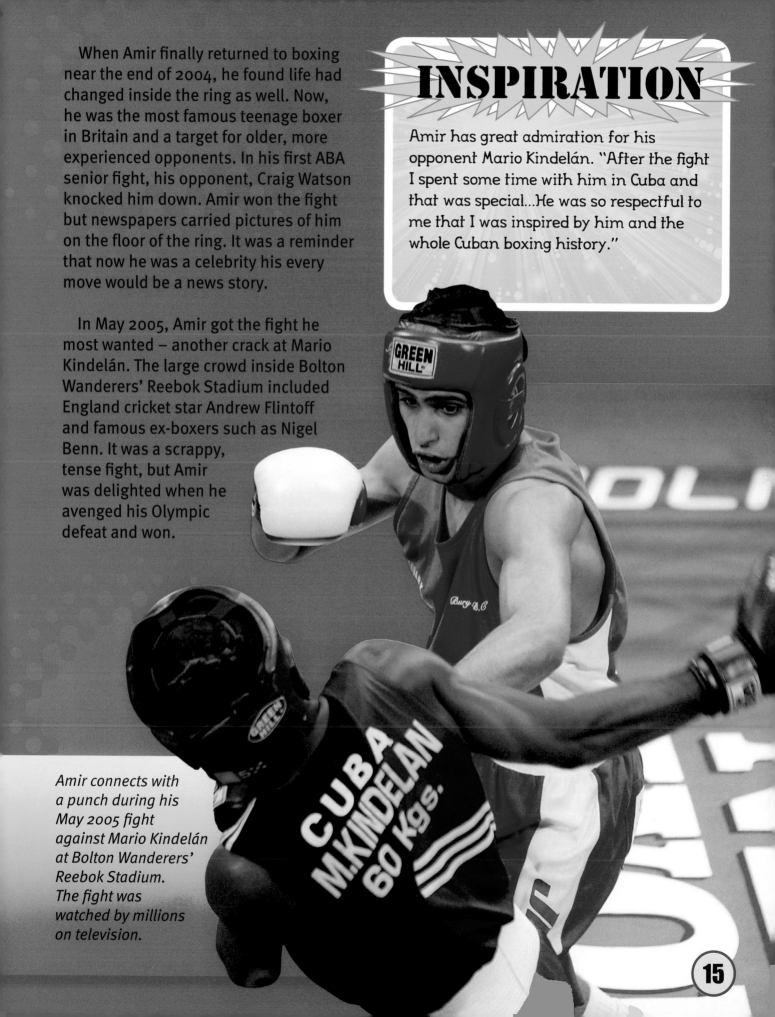

When Amir finally returned to boxing near the end of 2004, he found life had changed inside the ring as well. Now, he was the most famous teenage boxer in Britain and a target for older, more experienced opponents. In his first ABA senior fight, his opponent, Craig Watson knocked him down. Amir won the fight but newspapers carried pictures of him on the floor of the ring. It was a reminder that now he was a celebrity his every move would be a news story.

In May 2005, Amir got the fight he most wanted – another crack at Mario Kindelán. The large crowd inside Bolton Wanderers' Reebok Stadium included England cricket star Andrew Flintoff and famous ex-boxers such as Nigel Benn. It was a scrappy, tense fight, but Amir was delighted when he avenged his Olympic defeat and won.

INSPIRATION

Amir has great admiration for his opponent Mario Kindelán. "After the fight I spent some time with him in Cuba and that was special...He was so respectful to me that I was inspired by him and the whole Cuban boxing history."

Amir connects with a punch during his May 2005 fight against Mario Kindelán at Bolton Wanderers' Reebok Stadium. The fight was watched by millions on television.

Turning pro

The Mario Kindelán bout was Amir's last amateur fight. Many managers and **promoters** had made offers for Amir to turn professional. Amir, his family and Mick Jelley had debated whether he should stay an amateur and try to win a gold medal at the 2008 Olympics. In the end they decided he had achieved much as an amateur and should make the most of his fame and success by turning professional.

HONOURS BOARD

Amir was the youngest ever Olympic medallist to fight as a professional.

Amir and his family chose to sign with Frank Warren – an extremely experienced promoter who had managed Naseem Hamed, Ricky Hatton and Joe Calzaghe all to become world champions. It was a period of change for Amir, who was now working with trainer Oliver Harrison. Amir had to train hard and adapt to professional boxing's rules, which were different from the amateur code. He could no longer wear a vest or headguard, gloves were heavier and instead of four rounds, pro fights could last as long as 12 rounds.

Just before Amir's first professional fight he works hard in training with his coach, Oliver Harrison.

The referee steers Amir away after the boxer knocked his opponent Willie Limond to the floor at London's O2 Arena in 2007. It was Amir's first professional fight scheduled over 12 rounds and a tough test of Amir's boxing skills.

At first, though, Amir would be fighting shorter-length bouts to build up his experience. His first opponent, David Bailey, had newly turned professional himself with just seven fights. Amir said afterwards, "I was excited and nervous but as soon as the bell rang it went quiet in my head. It was just me and him." Amir demolished his opponent, with the referee stopping the fight in the first round. A succession of easy wins followed for Amir, although he and Frank Warren faced criticism that some of the opponents were not very challenging.

This was certainly not the case with his 13th fight, against Willie Limond for the Commonwealth lightweight title. Limond was a tough opponent and Amir found himself **knocked down** in the sixth round and in deep trouble.

In a thrilling comeback, he threw a flurry of ferocious punches in both the seventh and eighth rounds. Limond did not come out to fight the ninth. Amir had broken Limond's jaw and won his first professional title.

Amir's 11th professional fight against France's Mohammed Medjadji lasted less than a minute before Khan knocked him out.

Knocked down

Amir was enjoying life in and out of the ring, attending charity football matches with famous ex-stars and appearing at glitzy awards ceremonies and film premieres. He spent some of his income from fights and sponsorships on a Range Rover Vogue – a car big enough to carry Amir and the other five members of his family. He would later spend some more on a BMW sports car.

In 2008, Amir and his team decided on a change of trainer. Harrison was replaced with Jorge Rubio who had previously worked with Mario Kindelán. Amir's manager, Frank Warren, felt that Rubio would have the experience to take Amir towards a crack at a world title.

Amir's defence had been a little shaky in previous fights and Rubio worked on improving this in training. Rubio also suggested Amir's next opponent to Frank Warren who organised the fight to take place at the Manchester Evening News Arena. Amir would be facing the Colombian boxer, Bredis Prescott, who was known as a dangerous puncher. The fight sold out and 18,000 fans crammed into the Arena.

Amir works on his close punching speed and accuracy with his trainer Jorge Rubio before the Bredis Prescott fight.

As the bell to start the first round sounded, Amir rushed out and attacked Prescott. He felt strong and capable of knocking out his opponent, but he left his defence open and was struck by a powerful left **hook**. With his legs wobbling, Amir tried to defend but another left-handed punch by Prescott sent Amir crashing to the **canvas**.

He got to his feet only to be knocked down again. The referee had seen enough and stopped the fight. Amir Khan had been beaten in just 54 seconds of round one. He was devastated but straight after the fight he spoke to ringside reporters, admitted the mistakes he had made and vowed to bounce back.

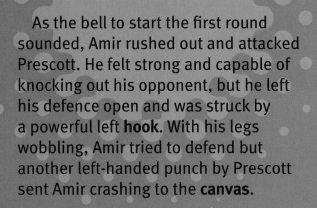

INSPIRATION

Amir learned from his defeat to Prescott. In a 2011 interview he said: "It made me change a few things in my life and made me realise who my real friends are. A lot of hangers-on drifted away."

TOP TIP

Part of the reason for Amir's defeat was his over-confidence that he could knock his opponent out quickly instead of boxing in his normal way. He vowed never to make that sort of error ever again.

Bredis Prescott knocks Amir to the floor to win their match in September, 2008. It was Amir's 19th professional fight and, until then, his only defeat.

Changing trainers

The Bredis Prescott bout was to be Jorge Rubio's only fight as Amir's trainer. Frank Warren stepped in, unhappy with what had happened, and Amir and his team began searching for a trainer who could rebuild his career towards a world title challenge.

That search led to the Wild Card Gym in Los Angeles, USA. There, Freddie Roach, an ex-boxer turned coach, had trained no fewer than 24 boxers who would go on to become world champions. These included boxing legends such as Oscar De La Hoya, Manny Pacquiao and Bernard Hopkins. Amir was immediately impressed with Roach's knowledge, enthusiasm and the way he worked.

INSPIRATION

Amir was thrilled share a gym with Manny Pacquiao. After beating Andreas Kotelnik in 2009, Amir said: "What a great inspiration he is for making me win this fight – the sparring with him, the working out... just talking to Manny Pacquiao took me to a different level."

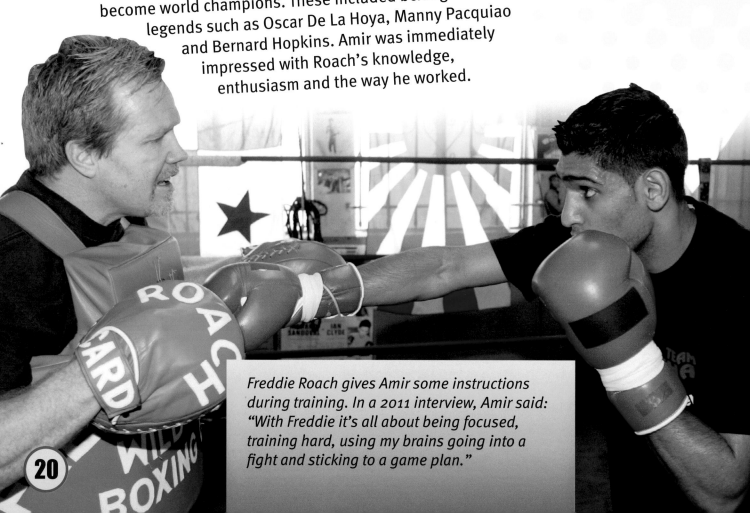

Freddie Roach gives Amir some instructions during training. In a 2011 interview, Amir said: "With Freddie it's all about being focused, training hard, using my brains going into a fight and sticking to a game plan."

The move to Los Angeles was not an easy one for Amir, though. He missed Bolton terribly and flew back whenever he could. But the gruelling training regime and no-excuses attitude at the Wild Card Gym really suited him. Mornings would start at 5.30am with warm ups and fitness and strength training involving intense sprints, runs up hills or sand dunes, swims and weight training. In the afternoons Amir worked in the gym and in the ring with Freddie Roach. This work would include ferocious **sparring** sessions where Amir and an opponent would wear protective gear but box seriously in the ring.

Amir started to feel the benefits of this new regime. He gained strength in his legs which helped him keep his balance better in the ring as he threw punches. He also learned more about the mental side of the sport and different tactics and ways of boxing from Freddie Roach. His first comeback fight after losing to Prescott was a resounding two-round defeat of Oisin Fagan. Two fights later, Amir would be world champion.

Wearing a head guard and trunk protector, Amir (left) spars in the famous Wild Card Gym in Los Angeles.

WOW!

When Amir is in training, his diet is carefully monitored. He eats a huge 6,300-6,800 calories each day but burns off over 5,000 of those in intense exercise.

Success in the ring

2009 proved to be a momentous year for Amir. Before he won the WBC world championship, he had a short but epic fight against former five-time world champion Marcos Antonio Barrera. The tough Mexican, a veteran of 70 professional fights, was Amir's stiffest challenge so far, but he won the fight in the fifth round, impressing his manager, Frank Warren who said: "He boxed brilliantly. It was a fantastic performance."

Despite the praise, Amir and his family announced that they were splitting from Frank Warren at the start of 2010. They signed up with Golden Boy Promotions, an American company run by boxing star Oscar De La Hoya.

Freddie Roach stands alongside Amir who wears both his WBC world championship belt and the International Boxing Federation (IBF) belt he won in 2011.

Shortly afterwards, Amir had his first US fight and defeated Paulie Malignaggi before dominating highly-rated Zab Judah in 2011, winning in the fifth round. His fight against Lamont Peterson, though, went all the way and was controversial with Amir deducted two points for pushing. Amir lost narrowly with two of the three judges giving it to Peterson by just one point. However, Peterson failed a drugs test and Amir was eventually reinstated as champion.

WOW!

In 2010, Amir won Boxing News' British Fighter of the Year and Fight Of The Year by the Boxing Writers Association of America.

Amir suffered a surprise defeat in 2012 to Danny Garcia, hitting the canvas three times before the referee stopped the fight. Smarting from the loss of his WBC world title, Amir changed trainers again, this time to Virgil Hunter and made a comeback against Carlos Molina in 2012 and backed up this success with a fight back in England, in 2013 where he defeated Mexican Julio Diaz.

The following year, saw Amir back in the United States for a fight versus American Luis Collazo for the WBA International and the WBC Silver welterweight titles. The bout went the full 12 rounds but all three judges made Amir the winner by a large margin. Amir repeated this dominant display in his next bout, landed over 240 punches whilst his opponent, Devon Alexander, only connected with 91. Another victory gave Amir a professional record by 2016 of 31 wins and three losses in his 34 fights, but he suffered a fourth defeat when fighting a heavier boxer, Saúl 'Canelo' Álvarez in May, 2016.

Amir knows that to succeed takes more than talent. It takes a lot of hard work and a positive mental attitude. He says: "You give up in your mind first. If your mind is strong you can push your body through the pain barrier. That's what you have to do to win."

Amir lands a punch on Lamont Peterson during their match in December 2011. More than 1,300 punches were thrown by the two boxers in the controversial fight.

A day in the life of Amir Khan

Amir is a wealthy sports star with large earnings from his winning fights as well as sponsorship deals and appearances. His family are involved in managing his money and have invested in over a dozen properties – houses and flats – which mean that Amir will still be wealthy after his career in boxing is over.

"I love my daughter to bits and becoming a father has made me much more emotional ... I think it's made me tougher, because now I'm fighting for my daughter. I'm doing it all for her now."

As a celebrity, Amir enjoys much of the attention he receives and attends events as varied as fashion shows and film premieres. He has shared the red carpet with stars from other sports as well as celebrities such as Sylvester Stallone and Arnold Schwarzenegger. But he has been careful not to let all the fame get to him and distract him from his goal of becoming a truly great boxer.

Amir and actor Hugh Jackman pose for photographs at the UK premiere of the film Real Steel in London in 2011.

Amir is extremely dedicated to training and boxing. When he's not in the gym or in the ring he enjoys spending as much time as possible in Bolton with his family and close friends. He likes watching movies and listening to music, but his great passion outside of boxing is cars. He has owned a variety of vehicles and has the personalised number plate BOX IIIG.

Amir and Faryal Makhdoom married in 2013 in New York then flew back to Bolton for a second celebration which included 4,000 guests. The couple's first child was born in May 2014, a daughter they named Lamaisah.

He has mostly avoided the scandal and bad behaviour that surrounds some other sports stars but in 2006, his love of fast cars got him into trouble. He was speeding in a 30mph zone and knocked down a pedestrian, breaking the person's leg. Amir was found guilty of careless driving in court in 2007. He was fined £1000 and banned from driving for six months. He later said of the incident: "It was the worst thing that's ever happened to me. I never want to harm anyone outside of a boxing ring."

WOW!

Amir's latest hobby is keeping tropical fish. He says that he finds them "really relaxing". Recently he spent a staggering £3,200 on a rare Gem Tang fish.

Charitable work

Amir is grateful to have had a loving, supportive family behind him since childhood. He knows that many children aren't so fortunate. As soon as his fame and fortune mounted after the Olympics, he was keen to make a difference and help out. He was made ambassador for the National Society for the Prevention of Cruelty to Children (NSPCC) in 2007 and in 2014 set up his own charitable organisation, The Amir Khan Foundation.

Amir feels passionately about young people and is concerned that some are not being looked after as well as they could be. "If you want to help young people, ask the young people what they need. Go to schools and assemblies and speak to them. Get their views, get involved with them. Young people know what they want to do in life and we need to support them."

Amir signs autographs as he arrives as a guest at the MOBO (Music of Black Origin) Awards in Glasgow, Scotland.

INSPIRATION

Amir finds being a role model to children inspiring. "It's interesting being looked up to by kids. It's a motivation for me, and it pushes me to go out and achieve more."

Amir has spent at least £700,000 of his own money to fund a boxing and community centre in Bolton called Gloves. It opened in 2008 and has more than 700 members – mostly young people who come in off the streets to train, get fit and learn about boxing. A number of famous boxers train in the gym including world champion Scott Quigg, a challenger Paul Smith and his brother Callum Smith, a potential future world champion.

Amir is also involved in charity efforts outside of Britain. In 2015 The Amir Khan Foundation worked to bring aid to refugees in Greece who had travelled there from Syria, Afghanistan and other countries. Food, clothes, hygiene items, tents and sleeping bags donated by the British public were shipped to Greece from the UK and given to the refugees, many of whom had very few belongings of their own. The charity is also building a village for orphans in The Gambia.

TOP TIP

Amir always tries to be friendly to fans, smiling for photos, signing autographs and chatting politely as it may be the only time that someone gets to meet him.

Amir and his brother, Haroon, appear in London to promote a 2010 appeal to help the victims of massive floods in Pakistan which have devastated large regions. Amir visited Pakistan in 2005 to help with the disaster relief work there after a large earthquake struck.

The impact of Amir Khan

An extremely talented and exciting fighter, Amir Khan's appearances and boxing bouts continue to attract large audiences as he moves up the boxing rankings. In the future, he hopes to seal big fights that will make his mark even more on the sport. "Money-wise, I could stop now," he said in an interview in 2011. "I've achieved my goals... The main ambition now is to become pound for pound the best fighter in the world."

Amir has some tough fights ahead to reach that goal but his impact already extends well beyond boxing. He is the UK's highest profile Muslim sportsman and he takes his responsibility as a role model for young people, not just young Asians in Britain, very seriously. Amir is involved in a number of charities and in 2011 was invited to a dinner at the **White House** for important Muslims in sport by US Secretary of State, Hillary Rodham Clinton.

HONOURS BOARD

In 2011, Amir won the Sports Personality of the Decade at the Lebara British Asian Sports Awards (BASA).

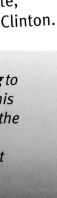

*Amir uses a **speed bag** to build up the speed of his punches in training at the Wild Card Gym shortly before his fight against Lamont Peterson.*

Amir has had to deal with ups and downs in the media spotlight including losing fights and being in court for driving offences, but he has learned from his mistakes and has won much praise for the way he handles himself. Amir was proud to receive an honorary degree in Manchester in 2016 and said, "I don't want to be seen as just a boxer but also a good person outside of the boxing ring as well."

Amir himself believes that: "I'm still the same person I was before I became famous" and remains close to his family and friends in Bolton. He is proud to be British and equally proud of his Asian background and Muslim faith. His career demonstrates how by dedication, hard work and in trusting good people around you can bring out the best in yourself.

TOP TIP

In an interview on his official website, Amir offered the following advice to young people. "Work hard towards your dreams and anything is achievable in life."

Amir has a pretend fight with a child at Parkinson Lane School in Halifax where he talked to pupils and opened a new extension to the school.

Have you got what it takes to be a boxing champion?

1) Do you enjoy sports which require strength or quick reactions like gymnastics, rugby or martial arts?
a) Yes, I play a lot of fast-moving sports as often as I can.
b) I play sports occasionally but more gentle ones like snooker and fishing.
c) No, I prefer watching sport to playing it.

2) When playing sport, how do you feel when you are hurt such as when you are tackled hard, fall or get a stitch from running?
a) I forget about it and start again straight away. It's all part of the sport.
b) I try to carry on but enjoy playing a lot less.
c) If that happened I would probably give up the sport.

3) Are you fit and do you tend to have a lot of energy?
a) Yes, I have loads of energy, with bags to spare.
b) Sometimes, I am energetic, but I could do with being fitter.
c) No, not really. I often feed tired and sluggish.

4) Do you get scared easily?
a) No, not at all. I am a bit of a daredevil.
b) Sometimes. Quite a few things make me nervous.
c) Yes, all the time. I get anxious and hate being frightened.

5) Can you be dedicated and make sacrifices in order to achieve a goal?
a) Yes, I can be single-minded and give up things I like to achieve an important target.
b) Maybe, but I'm not sure that I would want to spend all my spare time on one thing.
c) I'm into lots of different things and tend to switch from one to another. I don't think I'd want to just commit to one thing for a long time.

RESULTS

Mostly As: It sounds like you may really have the attitude and potential ability to enjoy boxing. Why not visit a local club to get a feel for the sport?

Mostly Bs: It sounds like you might want to stick to watching boxing and take part in a different sport yourself. Experiment with different sports to find one that suits your interest and sporting skills.

Mostly Cs: It doesn't sound like you are cut out for a career in boxing – well, not yet, anyway.

Glossary

ABA Short for Amateur Boxing Association, the organisation that runs amateur boxing in the UK.

amateur Not to be paid as a boxer to take part in fights.

autobiography A book about a person's life written by that person completely or in collaboration with another writer.

bout A boxing contest. Also known as a fight or match.

canvas The floor of the boxing ring.

hook A short sideways punch that is made with the arm bent at the elbow. It can be a very powerful punch.

jab A type of punch that is made as the arm straightens.

karate The Japanese art of weaponless self defence in which attacking and defensive movements are made with the hands and feet.

knocked down When a boxer is hit and parts of the body, other than the feet, touch the floor of the ring.

knock out When a referee stops a boxing bout and declares a boxer the winner if the opponent has been down for a count of ten.

podium The small stage that Olympic athletes stand on when they receive their gold, silver or bronze medals.

professional To be paid as a boxer to take part in fights.

promoter Someone who organises and puts on events featuring boxing bouts.

referee The official who stands inside the ring and makes sure that the boxers fight by the rules of the sport.

ring announcer The official who introduces the boxers before a bout and announces the result at the end of the fight.

round One of a series of periods, separated by rests, which make up a boxing bout.

sparring A type of boxing training in which a boxer fights against an opponent in the ring while wearing a helmet and other protective guards and clothing.

speed bag A small leather bag hanging in a gym that boxers hit to practise making quick punches.

trainer A coach and guide who helps prepare a boxer for each bout.

weight divisions A way of grouping boxers of similar size together, based on their weight. Each weight division, such as lightweight, middleweight and heavyweight, has a maximum weight which a boxer must be under just before a fight.

White House The official home of the President of the United States, in Washington DC.

Index